THINGS YOU'L HEAR *THEM** SAY

VOLUME ONE

THE ULTIMATE POLITICALLY INCORRECT HUMOR BOOK

*CELEBRITIES, JEWS, ORIENTALS, CATHOLICS, BLACKS, RACISTS, GAYS, REDNECKS, WASPS, BORN AGAINS, MEN, ITALIANS, LAWYERS, INDIANS (USA), FEMINISTS, DOCTORS, POLES, INDIANS (New Delhi), WOMEN, ARABS, PRISONERS, COWBOYS, SENIORS, ETC.

By: **ROSCOE BOULEVARD**

CCC PUBLICATIONS

Published by

CCC Publications
9725 Lurline Avenue
Chatsworth, CA 91311

Copyright ©1999 Roscoe Boulevard

All rights reserved by CCC Publications. No part of this book may be reproduced or transmitted in any form or by any means, electronic or mechanical, including photocopying, recording or by any information storage and retrieval system, without the written permission of the publisher, except where permitted by law.

For information address: CCC Publications; 9725 Lurline Avenue; Chatsworth, CA 91311

Manufactured in the United States of America

Cover ©1999 CCC Publications

Cover & interior production by Klaus Selbrede

ISBN: 1-57644-091-5

If your local U.S. bookstore is out of stock, copies of this book may be obtained by mailing check or money order for $6.95 per book (plus $2.75 to cover postage and handling) to: CCC Publications; 9725 Lurline Avenue; Chatsworth, CA 91311

Pre-publication Edition - 10/99

INTRODUCTION TO THEM.......

Everybody knows what "THEY" **DO** SAY & what "THEY" **WILL** SAY. But the eminent authors of this book thought it would be funny to write an important social novel about what "THEY" would **NEVER** SAY.

In the 30 years of painstaking research it took to write and investigate this breakthrough exposé, the authors have talked to, interviewed and orally abused millions of **"THEMS"** around the world and in their own neighborhood. Based on these interviews, many of these **"THEMS"** (against their will) agreed with us on the two important conclusions of our research:

1. They Would **NEVER** Say "These Things" and;

2. "These Things" They Would **NEVER** Say Would Be **FUNNY** In Print.

Based on these two critical findings, we have decided to allow CCC Publications to publish this book.

We hope you will agree with our decision and more importantly, that you will buy this book, as you may not be aware of the fact that all money the authors receive from the sale of **"THEM"** will be donated to charity to wipe out the greatest Jewish crippler of them all - WHIPLASH!

So, we ask you not only to buy this book (several copies, hopefully), but to share this masterpiece of literary history with your friends, family, loved-ones, probation officer, etcetera, no matter what kind of a "THEM" they are or would like to be.

In conclusion, these are things you'll NEVER hear **"THEM"** say. Maybe you wouldn't say them either, but thanks to us, you won't have to. We did it for you.

Thanks..... **M.A.C.**& **B.M.** aka

ROSCOE BOULEVARD

THINGS YOU'LL *NEVER* HEAR *THEM** SAY - VOLUME ONE

TABLE OF CONTENTS

CHAPTER ONE	....	CELEBRITIES	6
CHAPTER TWO	....	JEWS	10
CHAPTER THREE	....	BLACKS	13
CHAPTER FOUR	....	ORIENTALS	16
CHAPTER FIVE	....	CELEBRITIES 2	19
CHAPTER SIX	....	GAY MEN	22
CHAPTER SEVEN	....	ITALIANS	25
CHAPTER EIGHT	....	REDNECKS	28
CHAPTER NINE	....	CELEBRITIES 3	31
CHAPTER TEN	....	FEMINISTS	34
CHAPTER ELEVEN	....	COWBOYS	37
CHAPTER TWELVE	....	W.A.S.P.S	40
CHAPTER THIRTEEN	....	BORN AGAINS	42
CHAPTER FOURTEEN	....	CELEBRITIES 4	45
CHAPTER FIFTEEN	....	POLES	48

CHAPTER SIXTEEN	ARABS	51
CHAPTER SEVENTEEN	INDIANS (USA)	54
CHAPTER EIGHTEEN	KLANSMEN	57
CHAPTER NINETEEN	WOMEN	60
CHAPTER TWENTY	MEN	63
CHAPTER TWENTY-ONE	MEXICANS	66
CHAPTER TWENTY-TWO	PRISONERS	69
CHAPTER TWENTY-THREE	DOCTORS	72
CHAPTER TWENTY-FOUR	CELEBRITIES 5	75
CHAPTER TWENTY-FIVE	SENIORS	78
CHAPTER TWENTY-SIX	LAWYERS	81
CHAPTER TWENTY-SEVEN	INDIANS (NEW DELHI)	84
CHAPTER TWENTY-EIGHT	CATHOLICS	87
CHAPTER TWENTY-NINE	CELEBRITIES 6	90
CHAPTER THIRTY	MISC. THEM	93

CHAPTER ONE

THINGS YOU'LL *NEVER* HEAR
CELEBRITIES SAY
Part ONE

1. THINGS YOU'LL *NEVER* HEAR *CELEBRITIES* SAY - Part One

SYLVESTER STALLONE:

"To be or not to be..."

****

BILL CLINTON:

"Young lady, get out of my hotel room immediately — before I do something we'll both regret!"

****

POPE JOHN:

"Look at the hooters on Sister Theresa!"

****

1. THINGS YOU'LL *NEVER* HEAR *CELEBRITIES* SAY - Part One

MADONNA:

"No!"

****

ALEX TREBEK:

"I'm sorry, I can't answer that."

****

O.J. SIMPSON:

"Hi. This is O.J. Simpson with a public service message about Domestic Violence....."

****

1. THINGS YOU'LL *NEVER* HEAR *CELEBRITIES* SAY - Part One

ROBIN LEACH:

"With all your money, you live in this piece of crap?"

****

HILLARY CLINTON:

"Oh, come on, Newt. Just touch it. Bill will never know."

****

LARRY FLYNT:

"I'm sorry, Janice. We can't use you in the magazine. Your breasts are too big."

****

CHAPTER TWO

THINGS YOU'LL *NEVER* HEAR
JEWS SAY

2. THINGS YOU'LL *NEVER* HEAR *JEWS* SAY

"Excuse me...Thank You...Please..."

***

"Forgive me Father, for I have sinned."

***

JEWISH LANDLORD:
"That's OK, forget about the rent. Money isn't everything."

***

JEWISH HUSBAND:
"C'mon, Honey. No more oral sex tonight."

***

2. THINGS YOU'LL *NEVER* HEAR *JEWS* SAY

JEWISH PARENT:
"If you think your kids are stupid and ugly, you should see mine."

****

JEWISH PERSONAL INJURY ATTORNEY:
"Your honor, my client is feeling better today. We're withdrawing our lawsuit."

****

AT A RESTAURANT:
"Let me get that check."

****

ORTHODOX RABBI:
"More bacon, Cantor?"

****

CHAPTER THREE

THINGS YOU'LL *NEVER* HEAR
BLACKS SAY

3. THINGS YOU'LL *NEVER* HEAR *BLACKS* SAY

"Excuse me, sir. But did you drop this wallet?"

****

"Guilty, your Honor."

****

"No more wine for me, Bro'.
I've got to get up early for work."

****

BLACK ASTRONAUT:
"Yes, NASA." "No, NASA."

****

3. THINGS YOU'LL *NEVER* HEAR *BLACKS* SAY

"Hey! Turn that music down!!"

****

"Hoist the mainsail and trim the jib!"

****

"Of course it's paid for."

****

"Yeah, I was getting off the chairlift and boom! There went both of my skis!"

****

CHAPTER FOUR

THINGS YOU'LL *NEVER* HEAR
ORIENTALS SAY

---

4. THINGS YOU'LL *NEVER* HEAR *ORIENTALS* SAY

"I got a 100 on my driving test!"

****

"Does anybody here know how to load this camera?"

****

"You should see the boobs on my wife!"
"And boy, is my brother hung!"

****

4. THINGS YOU'LL *NEVER* HEAR *ORIENTALS* SAY

"I'm sorry, Mom. But you and Pop can't move in with us."

***

"I always travel alone."

***

"Wake up, Mei Ling. I'm *'jonesing'* for a knish and a pastrami on rye."

***

CHAPTER FIVE

THINGS YOU'LL *NEVER* HEAR
CELEBRITIES SAY
Part TWO

---

5. THINGS YOU'LL *NEVER* HEAR *CELEBRITIES* SAY - Part Two

LINDA TRIPP:

"Testing. One, two, three. Testing."

****

SHIRLEY MACLAINE:

"Hey, you only go around once...."

****

PETE ROSE:

"Five'll get you ten, Commissioner, I'm in the Hall of Fame next year."

****

5. THINGS YOU'LL *NEVER* HEAR *CELEBRITIES* SAY - Part Two

KATHY LEE GIFFORD:

"I'll forgive you Frank. But next time, I want to watch."

****

FRANK GIFFORD:

"Okay, Kathy. How 'bout next Saturday at eight?"

****

TED KENNEDY:

"Please, no more drinks for me. I'm driving."

****

CHAPTER SIX

THINGS YOU'LL *NEVER* HEAR
GAY MEN SAY

6. THINGS YOU'LL *NEVER* HEAR *GAY MEN* SAY

"He's not my type."

****

"These heels are so comfortable."

****

"No, I couldn't Troy. It's too big."

****

"I wonder if he has a sister?"

****

6. THINGS YOU'LL *NEVER* HEAR *GAY MEN* SAY

"Come on, guys. Just one sailor at a time, please!"

****

GAY DECORATOR:
"What this living room needs is loads of polka dots and day-glo bean bag furniture."

****

"I'm saving myself for someone special."

****

"I'll never do it that way."

****

CHAPTER SEVEN

THINGS YOU'LL *NEVER* HEAR
ITALIANS SAY

7. THINGS YOU'LL *NEVER* HEAR *ITALIANS* SAY

"Hey Tony! How do your wife and your mother stay so thin?"

****

"Yeah, that's me in the middle of the picture, holding the gun."

****

"Not pasta again!"

****

7. THINGS YOU'LL *NEVER* HEAR *ITALIANS* SAY

"Gino, I think you need some more brylcreme on your hair."

****

"So, what if you killed my two brothers. Why should I hold a grudge?"

****

"No? I don't believe it! We're out of olive oil?!"

****

CHAPTER EIGHT

THINGS YOU'LL *NEVER* HEAR
REDNECKS SAY

---

8. THINGS YOU'LL *NEVER* HEAR *REDNECKS* SAY

"You can't feed the dog *that!*"

****

AT THE MUSIC STORE:

"Excuse me, ma'am. Where's your Gangsta Rap section?"

****

"Do you have this shirt in anything besides flannel?"

****

"Screw the Super Bowl, Bubba. We're watchin' the ballet!"

****

8. THINGS YOU'LL *NEVER* HEAR *REDNECKS* SAY

"I can't eat that, Honey. It's got tire marks on it."

****

"I'm leaving you Emmy-Lou. But I want you to have my pickup and the dog."

****

"No thanks. One whiskey's my limit."

****

"Damnit Ma! We're out of Perrier again!!"

****

CHAPTER NINE

THINGS YOU'LL *NEVER* HEAR
CELEBRITIES SAY
Part THREE

9. THINGS YOU'LL *NEVER* HEAR *CELEBRITIES* SAY - Part Three

RUSH LIMBAUGH:
"I apologize for interrupting you."

****

WHOOPI GOLDBERG:
"I'm not just another pretty face in Hollywood."

****

RICHARD SIMMONS:
"Can you believe it? My wife's pregnant AGAIN!"

****

9. THINGS YOU'LL *NEVER* HEAR *CELEBRITIES* SAY - Part Three

SNOOP DOGGY DOG
"The cops are your friends, And all women are cool. So don't kill or do drugs, Just stay in da' school."

****

MARIO ANDRETTI:
"Why don't you drive, Honey."

****

DAVE LETTERMAN
"Let me call Jay. If he thinks it's funny, it stays in."

****

CHAPTER TEN

THINGS YOU'LL *NEVER* HEAR *FEMINISTS* SAY

10. THINGS YOU'LL *NEVER* HEAR *FEMINISTS* SAY

"No problem, Honey, I'll sleep on the wet spot."

****

"Do twice the work for half the money?....Okay by me."

****

"You just lie there, Steve. I'll get you another beer."

****

10. THINGS YOU'LL *NEVER* HEAR *FEMINISTS* SAY

"I never met a man I didn't like."

****

"You've got to look for the good in your man."

****

"Sure, there's no doubt about it. Some women just need a good slap once in a while."

****

CHAPTER ELEVEN

THINGS YOU'LL *NEVER* HEAR
COWBOYS SAY

11. THINGS YOU'LL *NEVER* HEAR *COWBOYS* SAY

"I'm going to pass, Honey, I just can't drink another beer."

****

"I'm sorry, Tex, but I'm too stressed out to eat BBQ."

****

IN THE BUNK HOUSE:
"Wow, Red! Nice sheets!"

****

11. THINGS YOU'LL *NEVER* HEAR *COWBOYS* SAY

AT THE CHUCK WAGON:

"More paté, Cookie, and pile on the tofu."

****

"Pack up the kids and the trailer, Honey. We're moving to Connecticut."

****

"I tell you, Billy-Bob. If we could get more gays and lawyers to move here, Texas would be a helluva state."

****

CHAPTER TWELVE

THINGS YOU'LL *NEVER* HEAR
W.A.S.P.S SAY

12. THINGS YOU'LL *NEVER* HEAR *WASPS* SAY

"Hey, Al! Ya' wanna take a look at this before I flush it?"

****

"Yes, operator. Bunny and I would like to renew our subscriptions to Ebony and Jet."

****

"Okay, kids. Who took Daddy's crack money?"

****

"Gimme five, homey!"

****

CHAPTER THIRTEEN

THINGS YOU'LL *NEVER* HEAR
BORN AGAINS SAY

13. **THINGS YOU'LL *NEVER* HEAR *BORN AGAINS* SAY**

"I'll be damned! Darwin was right."

****

"Nice sermon, Reverend.
But I think the atheists deserve equal time."

****

"Mom and Dad, I'd like you to meet
my fiancé, Rabbi Goldstein."

****

13. THINGS YOU'LL *NEVER* HEAR *BORN AGAINS* SAY

"Say, Deacon. Will you and the missus be attending the Good Friday Orgy again this year?"

****

"Well, you can't always rely on Scripture, Parson. Maybe the Disciples were gay."

****

"Two Apostles go into a bar...."

****

CHAPTER FOURTEEN

THINGS YOU'LL *NEVER* HEAR
CELEBRITIES SAY
Part FOUR

---

14. THINGS YOU'LL *NEVER* HEAR *CELEBRITIES* SAY - Part Four

MICHAEL JORDAN:
"Say, Dennis. Can I borrow your eyeliner?"
KARL MALONE:
"Say, Dennis. Can I use it when Michael's finished?"
DENNIS RODMAN:
"Eyeliner? What eyeliner?"

****

DR. KERVORKIAN:
"Call me in the morning."

****

MICKEY ROURKE:
"Pass the soap."

****

14. THINGS YOU'LL *NEVER* HEAR *CELEBRITIES* SAY - Part Four

QUEEN ELIZABETH:
"Oh look, Phil! K-Mart is having a sale on hats!"

***

BILL GATES:
"Uh, you want fries with that?"

***

CHER:
"I can't wear that skimpy thing in public!"

***

CHAPTER FIFTEEN

THINGS YOU'LL *NEVER* HEAR *POLES* SAY

15. THINGS YOU'LL *NEVER* HEAR *POLES* SAY

"Oh, yeah. I get it!"

****

"Let me think about it."

****

"It's not easy being smarter than everybody else."

****

15. THINGS YOU'LL *NEVER* HEAR *POLES* SAY

"The square of the hypotenuse is equal to the sum of the squares of the other two sides."

****

"Somebody turn off that damn polka music!"

****

"Yes, I am and my brother's a rocket scientist too."

****

CHAPTER SIXTEEN

THINGS YOU'LL *NEVER* HEAR
ARABS SAY

16. THINGS YOU'LL *NEVER* HEAR *ARABS* SAY

"Pass the shampoo, Wazir."

****

"You do it, Amir. That camel's too ugly for me."

****

"Boy, that was some square dance at the Mosque last night, huh?"

****

"Don't fire Omar! You might hit a Jew!"

****

16. **THINGS YOU'LL *NEVER* HEAR *ARABS* SAY**

IN THE BAZAAR:

"Is this the smallest bikini you have?"

****

"...And this is my daughter Fatima.
Winner of the 'wet veil contest'."

****

"Screw Ramadan! Did somebody say McDonalds?"

****

"Another matzoh ball, Ayatolla?"

****

CHAPTER SEVENTEEN

THINGS YOU'LL *NEVER* HEAR
INDIANS *(USA)* SAY

_17._ THINGS YOU'LL _NEVER_ HEAR _INDIANS (USA)_ SAY

"Sorry, white eyes, the casino's closed."

****

AT THE SOUVENIR STAND:

"Give me two Cleveland Indian caps, three Atlanta Braves tomahawks and one of those Redskin tee shirts, please."

****

"We gave our child a Jewish name, 'White Fish'."

****

17. THINGS YOU'LL *NEVER* HEAR *INDIANS (USA)* SAY

"Personally, I don't mind Beverly Hills, Running Bear, but give me the reservation any day."

****

"My name is Doctor John 'Red Cloud' Jensen. But you can call me 'Tonto'."

****

"C'mon, White Eagle, take off the headdress. Feathers are for sissies!"

****

CHAPTER EIGHTEEN

THINGS YOU'LL *NEVER* HEAR
KLANSMEN SAY

18. THINGS YOU'LL *NEVER* HEAR *KLANSMEN* SAY

"Come on in, Leroy. My daughter will be right down."

****

"You know, Verne, call me sentimental, but Black really IS beautiful."

****

"We've got nothing to hide, Ray. I say we take off the hoods and let 'em see who we really are!"

****

18. **THINGS YOU'LL *NEVER* HEAR *KLANSMEN* SAY**

"Son-of-a-bitch!! Does anybody here know how to light this fuse?"

****

"We can't burn that! It's a Church for Chrissakes!"

****

"So what if he's black, Billy-Joe. Ya' know we always need new members."

****

CHAPTER NINETEEN

THINGS YOU'LL *NEVER* HEAR WOMEN SAY

19. THINGS YOU'LL *NEVER* HEAR *WOMEN* SAY

"I want our relationship to be more physical! I'm tired of just being friends."

****

"This diamond is WAY too big!"

****

"Go ahead and leave the toilet seat up. It's easier to douche that way."

****

19. THINGS YOU'LL *NEVER* HEAR *WOMEN* SAY

"Wow, Bill! It really is 14 inches!"

****

"Does this make my butt look too small?"

****

"Hey, Honey, get a whiff of that one!"

****

"I'm absolutely wrong. You must be right."

****

CHAPTER TWENTY

THINGS YOU'LL *NEVER* HEAR *MEN* SAY

20. THINGS YOU'LL *NEVER* HEAR *MEN* SAY

"Sex is not that important to me.
Sometimes I just want to be held."

****

"Sure, Honey. I would absolutely LOVE
to wear a condom."

****

"We haven't been to the mall for ages.
Let's go shopping so I can hold your purse."

****

20. THINGS YOU'LL *NEVER* HEAR *MEN* SAY

"Screw Monday Night Football!
Let's watch the Home Shopping Channel."

****

"While I'm up Darling, can I get you anything
from the kitchen?"

****

"I think we're lost. We better pull
over and ask for directions."

****

CHAPTER TWENTY-ONE

THINGS YOU'LL *NEVER* HEAR
MEXICANS SAY

21. THINGS YOU'LL *NEVER* HEAR *MEXICANS* SAY

"Not tonight, Maria. I'm out of rubbers."

****

"I'm telling you, Manuel, forget Merrill Lynch. Go with Smith Barney."

****

AT THE AIRPORT:

"Is this the departure gate to Monaco?"

****

"No, I am not Spanish. I'm a Mexican — and proud of it!"

****

21. THINGS YOU'LL *NEVER* HEAR *MEXICANS* SAY

"Can't help you out, Pedro. I don't have any jumper cables."

****

"I can't eat this. Salsa gives me heartburn."

****

"Why go North, Jose? Mexico has everything you'd ever want or need!"

****

CHAPTER TWENTY-TWO

THINGS YOU'LL *NEVER* HEAR
PRISONERS SAY

22. THINGS YOU'LL *NEVER* HEAR *PRISONERS* SAY

"Jeez, Lefty, where'd the year go?"

****

"Just bend over, Warden. I'll be gentle."

****

DEATH ROW INMATE:

"My only regret is that I'll never hear another Robert Goulet album."

****

21. THINGS YOU'LL *NEVER* HEAR *PRISONERS* SAY

"You dropped the soap, Spike. I'll get it."

***

IN THE MESS HALL:

"You call this Quiche!?"

***

ON DEATH ROW:

"For my last meal I'd like the Weight Watcher's plate with a diet soda."

***

CHAPTER TWENTY-THREE

THINGS YOU'LL *NEVER* HEAR
DOCTORS SAY

23. THINGS YOU'LL *NEVER* HEAR *DOCTORS* SAY

"To tell you the truth, I specialize in diseases of the rich."

****

PSYCHIATRIST:
"That's the most disgusting story I ever heard.
Get the hell out of my office!"

****

"If you have to wait more than 5 minutes,
your office visit is free."

****

"I really think you need to see a Chiropractor."

****

23. THINGS YOU'LL *NEVER* HEAR *DOCTORS* SAY

PSYCHIATRIST:
"You're cured. You don't need me anymore."

***

"Forget the prescription. There's an inexpensive herb you can get at any health food store."

***

"Don't worry about paying my fee. Your HMO insurance covers everything."

***

"I think getting a second opinion is a very wise idea."

***

CHAPTER TWENTY-FOUR

THINGS YOU'LL *NEVER* HEAR
CELEBRITIES SAY
Part FIVE

24. THINGS YOU'LL *NEVER* HEAR *CELEBRITIES* SAY - Part Five

MONICA LEWINSKY:

"If you want to know the truth, I think Ken Starr's is a lot bigger than Bill's."

****

DONNIE & MARIE OSMOND:

"We're through with drugs! And this time we mean it!!"

****

REVEREND BILLY GRAHAM:

"How much for all night?"

****

24. THINGS YOU'LL *NEVER* HEAR *CELEBRITIES* SAY - Part Five

CHEF WOLFGANG PUCK:

"If you really want to know, the secret to my special sauce is just wee pinch of monkey dung."

****

MRS. REGIS PHILBIN:

"It's not easy being married to a talented star."

****

JOAN RIVERS

"I can't say that! Cher will be devastated!"

****

CHAPTER TWENTY-FIVE

THINGS YOU'LL *NEVER* HEAR *SENIORS* SAY

25. THINGS YOU'LL *NEVER* HEAR *SENIORS* SAY

AFTER EATING:

"Race you to the car, Shirley."

****

AT THE RETIREMENT HOME:

"Sure, I remember YOU."

****

"Who needs savings or family help?
We can make it on our Social Security."

****

25. THINGS YOU'LL *NEVER* HEAR *SENIORS* SAY

"I wish my kids wouldn't visit me so much."

****

"Honey, have you seen my skate board?"

****

"I love all music. But rap's my favorite."

****

"Absolutely no complaints. They really take great care of me here at the rest home."

****

CHAPTER TWENTY-SIX

THINGS YOU'LL *NEVER* HEAR
LAWYERS SAY

26. THINGS YOU'LL *NEVER* HEAR *LAWYERS* SAY

"I'm a licensed attorney, sir.
I won't stoop *that* low."

****

"I'm sorry, but since you told me the truth about what you did, no amount of money could convince me to defend you now."

****

"Here's a refund check.
I discovered I over-billed you."

****

26. THINGS YOU'LL *NEVER* HEAR *LAWYERS* SAY

"I couldn't. It would be unethical."

****

"Bill, I don't think we should sue Dr. Kirkland just because your wife lost a couple of organs."

****

"Ladies and gentlemen of the jury, my client is clearly guilty."

****

CHAPTER TWENTY-SEVEN

THINGS YOU'LL *NEVER* HEAR
INDIANS (New Delhi) SAY

27. THINGS YOU'LL *NEVER* HEAR *INDIANS* (New Delhi) SAY

"Does curry and rice come with the beef ribs?"

****

"I can't work at the 7-11. It's against my religion."

****

"Two Hindus go into a bar..."

****

27. THINGS YOU'LL *NEVER* HEAR *INDIANS* (New Delhi) SAY

"Some of my best friends are Pakistanis."

****

"Sacred, shmacred! A river's a river!"

****

"Speak English, Dammit!!"

****

CHAPTER TWENTY-EIGHT

THINGS YOU'LL *NEVER* HEAR
CATHOLICS SAY

28. THINGS YOU'LL *NEVER* HEAR *CATHOLICS* SAY

PARENTS OF AN ALTAR BOY:

"Sure, Monsignor, Johnny can sleep over at Father Duffy's again tonight."

****

PRIEST:

"That's B.S. What does the Pope know anyway?"

****

"Great sermon, Father Alice!"

****

28. THINGS YOU'LL *NEVER* HEAR *CATHOLICS* SAY

"Christmas is about Santa Claus. Period!"

****

"I'm glad you agree, Sister Mary. An abortion would be the best thing."

****

"Just because I'm Catholic, Father, doesn't mean that I have to raise my children Catholic."

****

CHAPTER TWENTY-NINE

THINGS YOU'LL *NEVER* HEAR
CELEBRITIES SAY
Part SIX

29. THINGS YOU'LL *NEVER* HEAR *CELEBRITIES* SAY - Part Six

PAULY SHORE:

"First of all, I would like to thank the academy..."

****

MICHAEL JACKSON:

"I think you're too young for me, Bobby. Let's ask your parents."

****

JANET RENO:

"If I had known politics would be this difficult, I would've stayed a swim suit model."

****

29. THINGS YOU'LL *NEVER* HEAR *CELEBRITIES* SAY - Part Six

REVEREND JESSE JACKSON:
"Some of my best friends are black."

****

KEITH RICHARDS:
"Yeah, but I didn't inhale."

****

BOB VILA:
"Welcome, to my new show, 'This Old Whorehouse'."

****

CHAPTER THIRTY

THINGS YOU'LL *NEVER* HEAR *THEM*** SAY

**MISCELLANEOUS THEMS

30. THINGS YOU'LL *NEVER* HEAR Miscellaneous "THEM" SAY

AA MEETING SPEAKER:
"For tonight's meeting we have a two-drink minimum."

***

MILITARY MAN:
"General, are you sure we can take this orphanage without using napalm, sir?"

***

PRISON WARDEN:
"Okay guys, you can keep the drugs, but the hookers have to be out of here by midnight."

***

30. THINGS YOU'LL *NEVER* HEAR Miscellaneous *"THEM"* SAY

AIRLINE PASSENGER:
"I don't know about you Fred, but I fly for the food and service."

****

MORMON:
"Okay! Belly up to the bar, boys. The drinks are on me."

****

POLITICIAN:
"In conclusion..."

****

AN ACCORDION PLAYER:
"No another booking! I've got to get a beeper."

****

30. THINGS YOU'LL *NEVER* HEAR *Miscellaneous* "THEM" SAY

IRISHMAN:
"No thank you. I don't drink anymore."

****

PROCTOLOGIST:
"I'm going to try to be as gentle as possible."

****

HOLLYWOOD AGENT:
"Forget my commission. I'm just glad you're working!"

****

ETHIOPIAN:
"Would you like an after dinner mint?"

****